Counseling Ch[ildren with] Behavio[r Problems]

by Steve Johnson, PhD

Author's Note

Copyright © 2013 by Steve A. Johnson. All rights reserved.

This publication is designed to provide accurate and authoritative information in regard to the subject matter covered. It is sold with the understanding that the author is not engaged in rendering psychological, financial, legal, or other professional services. If expert assistance or counseling is needed, the services of a competent professional should be sought.

No part of this book may be reproduced, stored in a retrieval system, or transmitted, in any form or by any means, electronic, mechanical, photocopying, microfilming, recording, or otherwise.

Please Note

This book is a combination of two volumes in the REBT and Spiritual Growth Series that have appeared in Kindle form through Amazon.com. Therefore, there is some repetition in the explanation of the ABC model of care and counseling in the two sections of this book. The explanations are not identical but some of the same content is explained in different language.

The author thought it was important enough to have some repetition for the reader to fully grasp that model, and in the second part of the book to see in more detail how the model could be applied to prayer.

I apologize to those readers who may not need such repetition

Contents

Introduction 6
    The Genesis of REBT 6
    Irrational Beliefs 8
    Rational Beliefs 10
    REBT and Scripture 11
    Demandingness 14
    Awfulizing 16
    Low Frustration Tolerance (LFT) 17
    Self- and Other-Downing 18
    Is REBT too Self-Centered? 20
    Special Problems Working with Christian Clients 22
    Unconditional Self Acceptance (USA) vs. Self-Rating 24
    Religious Interventions within an REBT Framework 26

Prayer in More Depth 41
    Introduction 41
    The Parts of a Dynamic Prayer 46
    Composing a Dynamic Prayer 52
    Sample Dynamic Prayer 53
    Using This Form of Prayer in the Church 54
    Prayer for Overcoming Anxious Spirit 56
    Prayer for an Overcoming an Angry Spirit 57
    Prayer for Overcoming a Guilty Spirit 58
    Prayer for Transcending Spiritual Dryness 59
    Prayer for Overcoming Spiritual Doubts 60

Prayer for Ending Frustration with Christians/Church 61

Prayer When Experiencing a Major Loss 62

Prayer for Solutions to Family Problems 63

Prayer for Dealing with Chronic Health Problems 64

Prayer to Overcome a Judgmental Spirit 65

Prayer When Feeling Hurt about the Past 66

Prayer for Dealing with a Bad Work Environment 67

Prayer for Overcoming Sin and Temptation 68

Prayer for Those Who Had an Abortion 69

Prayer to Overcome Resentment 70

Prayer for Overcoming Financial Challenges 71

Prayers When Coveting Someone Else's Possessions 72

Prayers to Stop Gossiping 73

Prayer for Our Political Leaders 74

Prayer to Overcome a Poor Attitude Toward Non-Christians 75

Conclusion 76

Counseling Christians for Mental, Emotional, Behavioral, and Spiritual Health

Introduction

Albert Ellis, the founder of Rational Emotive Behavior Therapy (REBT) and what some have called the grandfather of all forms of cognitive behavior therapy, often said, "The deepest, most profound change that you can help clients achieve is to help them change their philosophy of life."

St. Paul, in his second letter to the Corinthians, wrote:

From now on, therefore we regard no one from a human point of view; even though we once knew Christ from a human point of view, we know him no longer in that way. So if anyone is in Christ, there is a new creation; everything old has passed away; see, everything has become new. (II Corinthians 5:16-17)

Since one's philosophy of life is a "way of seeing" life, the world, others, and the self, both Ellis and St. Paul are advocating a profound change in one's "way of seeing," in other words, one's point of view or set of beliefs that one holds about life.

In this publication, I will suggest ways that Christian beliefs and practices can be incorporated into the practice of REBT/CBT to help Christian clients adopt a new "way of seeing," so they can experience themselves as a "new creation" with fewer emotional disturbances and self-defeating behaviors. I will also enumerate some of the more difficult issues that arise in psychotherapy with Christian clients and offer some possible ways to respond to these difficult issues.

The Genesis of REBT

Many, if not most, people operate out of an erroneous emotional equation. This equation is "Events cause emotions and behaviors."

It really isn't surprising that we hold such an erroneous equation. For example, let us say that George believes that he is called by God to become an ordained minister. Holding that belief, he applies for entrance to several seminaries, but he is turned down by all of them. Immediately upon learning about being rejected by them all, George feels depressed. The depression happens so quickly that it is natural that later when a friend asks him why he is so down, George says, "I am depressed because I just got rejected from seminary." George operates out of an erroneous emotional equation; he assumes that it is the event, namely, getting rejected by all the seminaries, that caused his depression.

Albert Ellis found a line in Epictetus' Enchiridion that was a corrective to the erroneous emotional equation. That line, "People are disturbed not by things, but by the view they take of them," served as one of the inspirations for Ellis's ABC model of emotional disturbance. Ellis held that when an activating event occurs (hereafter referred to as A), it triggers a belief or set of beliefs about the event (such beliefs are hereafter referred to as B), which largely contributes to what we feel and do (hereafter referred to as C).

In our example, when all the seminaries rejected George (A), the following set of beliefs (B) may have been triggered:

+I ought to have been accepted into a seminary.
+I will never be an ordained minister, and that is awful.
+I am a failure as a person for being rejected by the seminaries.

That set of beliefs is what largely led George to feel depressed. Now, let us say that George held a different set of beliefs, such as the following:

+I wish I had been accepted into a seminary.
+I don't like the fact that I may never be an ordained minister, but it isn't really a catastrophe. God still love me, and I can still have a meaningful life and most likely find

another form of ministry through which I can serve others and God

+I did fail at getting accepted into a seminary, but I am not a failure as a human or as a Christian.

With George's first set of beliefs he made himself feel depressed, and as a result, his energy could not go into thinking of other ways to fulfill what he believed to be his call to the ministry. However, had he held the second set of beliefs, George might have felt sad and disappointed that he did not get accepted into a seminary, but not so depressed that he lost sight of other more helpful and comforting beliefs. The second set of beliefs also permitted him to use his energy to begin to take steps to find another form of ministry that he might experience as fulfilling. So the strategy of REBT is to have people change their unhelpful or irrational beliefs to more rational or functional beliefs, so they can feel and act in more appropriate and helpful ways to achieve their life goals.

Irrational Beliefs

F.P. Ramsey, a student of Wittgenstein, poetically defined beliefs as "a map and something by which we steer" (Armstrong, 1973). Irrational beliefs create a wild fanciful map that does not correspond to social reality, and when we try to steer by it, we encounter all kinds of life problems. Rational beliefs create a map that more closely corresponds to social reality, and more important, when we steer by it, we encounter fewer problems. Thus beliefs are not merely cognitive. Instead, as Ramsey points out, they have an action component associated with them: that is, they frequently indicate a tendency to act in a particular way under certain conditions. C.S. Peirce, the father of American pragmatism, noted that beliefs are not only a tendency to act in a particular way, but they are held for emotional reasons, namely, to reduce or dispel the problem of doubt (1955). This view is similar to Ellis's view that cognition, action, and emotion are inextricably interrelated. When we *think*, we feel and have a tendency to act. When we *act*, we feel and hold beliefs. When we *feel*, we tend to act in particular ways due to the beliefs behind the feelings.

REBT holds that an irrational belief actually has at least two irrational parts: a core demand and a derivative. A core demand usually contains absolutistic words such as "must," "absolutely should," "ought," "need," or "have to." For example, "I must be accepted into a seminary." "You ought to love me unconditionally," "Life should be easier than it is," "The world has to be fair," and "I need you in my life."

A derivative takes one of the following four forms:

> **+Awfulizing:** X is awful, terrible, horrible, catastrophic, or as bad as it could possibly be.
> **+Low Frustration Tolerance (LFT):** I can't stand X, X is too much. X is intolerable or unbearable.
> **+Self-Downing:** I am no good, worthless, useless, an utter failure, beyond help or hope, damnable, devoid of value.
> **+Other-Downing:** You are no good, worthless, useless, an utter failure, beyond help or hope, damnable, devoid of value.

A core demand is usually combined with one or more derivatives:

> +I must get accepted into seminary, and it is awful if I don't. (Demand + Awfulizing)
> +I must get accepted into seminary, and I couldn't stand it if I didn't. (Demand + LFT)
> +I must get accepted into seminary, and I'm a failure if I don't. (Demand + Self-Downing)
> +I must get accepted into seminary, and the seminary admissions committee is damnable if it doesn't accept me. (Demand + Other-Downing)

Note that each of these pairs causes some unhelpful negative emotion. For example, the demand plus the other-downing might lead to anger at the admissions committee; the demand plus the self-downing might lead to depression; and the demand plus the LFT might lead to anxiety. Since anger, depression, and anxiety are likely to interfere with people's achieving their life goals, it is in their best interest to change their core irrational demands and associated derivatives.

Rational Beliefs

Of course, rational beliefs are rational alternatives to irrational core demands and derivatives. The rational alternative to a core demand is a statement of want, preference, or desire. For example, the rational alternative to "I must get accepted into seminary" is "I would like to get accepted," or "I want to get accepted into seminary." REBT does not aim at eliminating desires, wishes, or preferences, only at eliminating the demands. A desire or preference accepts that the world, life, the self, or others are the way they are. A demand, on the other hand, frequently does not correspond to social reality, and is therefore likely to cause the individual to feel or act in unhelpful ways.

Irrational derivatives also have rational alternatives:

> +**Rational alternative to Awfulizing:** I don't like X and it may be really bad, but it isn't a catastrophe.
> +**Rational alternative to LFT:** I don't like X and it certainly isn't pleasant, but it isn't unbearable.
> +**Rational alternative to Self-Downing:** I may not have acted in the way I would like, but that doesn't make me an utter failure as a human.
> +**Rational alternative to Other-Downing:** You may not have acted in the way I wish you had, but you are not utterly damnable.

REBT helps us minimize the occurrence of the unhelpful negative emotions and self-sabotaging actions by giving us a method by which we can recognize our irrational beliefs, demonstrate to ourselves why they are irrational (dispute them), and then replace them with rational alternatives. In other words, REBT helps individuals achieve a radically new and more effective "way of seeing."

REBT and Scripture

Ellis referred to Epictetus to describe the role of belief in human emotional disturbance. An even older source, namely, the book, of Proverbs in the Old Testament, says essentially the same thing: "As one thinks in one's heart, so is one." For this reason, some writers have concluded, "[REBT] is based on a thoroughly biblical principle, the importance of what one things" (Lawrence, 1987).

Several places in Scripture demonstrate that beliefs, not events, cause actions and feelings. Consider the Old Testament story of Jonah. In the beginning of the story, God asks Jonah to go to Ninevah and speak against the wickedness of the Ninevites. Since the Ninevites were the traditional enemy, and Jonah does not relish the thought of standing in the midst of his enemies and telling them they act wickedly, Jonah avoids doing what God asks. Instead, Jonah escapes on a ship headed toward Tarshish but he ends up being thrown overboard by the ship's crew and swallowed by a great fish. Inside the fish, Jonah repents. He seems to be cured of his self-defeating behavior of not doing what God asks, but we soon discover that a deeper problem, "a demand," lurks in his psyche and continues to cause him emotional and behavioral problems.

When the fish releases Jonah, God again tells Jonah to go to Ninevah and preach that the great city will be overthrown for its wickedness. This time Jonah goes and, in fact, does such a good job of preaching that the Ninevites repent and God spares them. Jonah is furious; he was internally demanding that God punish the Ninevites. God, very much like an REBT therapist, says, "Do you do well to be angry?" In other words, God is asking how Jonah's demand is helping Jonah. Jonah doesn't respond, but he escapes to the east of the city in the hope that God will change and destroy Ninevah.

God does not destroy Ninevah, but does send a plant to give Jonah shade from the scorching heat. However, as Jonah becomes accustomed to the shade, God sends a worm to destroy the plant. Jonah is angry again, probably telling himself that he can't stand the loss of the plant and the resultant heat. He then declares, "It is better for me to die than to live." Again, God essentially says, "How is this helping you?" Jonah still doesn't get it, so God gives him a live analogy. God reminds Jonah that Jonah pities the loss of the plant for which he did nothing, so why can't God legitimately pity Ninevah with its more than 120,000 people who repented?

The story of Jonah shows how Jonah's beliefs caused him to engage in avoidance of his responsibility, which got him in all kinds of trouble, and to experience a rage so unpleasant that Jonah wanted to die. God shows the inadequacy of those beliefs by asking Jonah how the irrational beliefs are helping him and by offering a concrete analogy that demonstrates the illogical and unjust nature of Jonah's beliefs.

Another very clear demonstration of REBT in Scripture is Jeremiah in Lamentations 3. Note the hopelessness, misery, distress, bitterness, anguish, sense of being constrained or trapped, fear, despair, depression, and physical symptoms in the following passages:

I am the man who has seen affliction under the rod of his wrath; He has driven and brought me into darkness without any light; Surely against me he turns his hand again and again the whole day long. He has made my flesh and my skin waste away, and broken my bones. He has besieged and enveloped me with bitterness and tribulation; He has made me dwell in darkness like the dead of long ago. He has walled me about so that I cannot escape; He has put heavy chains on me; Though I call and cry for help, He shuts out my prayer; He has blocked my ways with hewn stones, He has made my paths crooked. He is to me like a bear lying in wait, like a lion in hiding; He led me off my way and tore me to pieces; He has made me desolate; He bent his bow and set me as a mark for his arrow.

He drove into my heart the arrows of his quiver. I have become the laughingstock of all peoples, the burden of their songs all day long. He has filled me with bitterness, He has sated me with wormwood. He has made my teeth grind on gravel, and made me cower in ashes; My soul is bereft of peace, I have forgotten what happiness is. So I say, "Gone is my glory, and my expectation from the Lord." Remember my affliction and my bitterness, the wormwood and the gall!

As David Stoop has pointed out, the reason Jeremiah experiences this long list of extremely unpleasant feelings is revealed in the following verse: "My soul continually thinks of it and is bowed down within me" (1997, p. 33). Jeremiah feels the way he feels primarily because he keeps dwelling on his belief that his state of affairs is truly awful. As he continues to tell himself how awful it is, he continues to feel awful!

What permits Jeremiah to eventually escape his misery? The answer is in the next verse: But this I call to mind, and therefore I have hope. Jeremiah replaces his depression and anger with hope because he begins to think differently; he embraces a new way of seeing and thinking about his situation. He says,

The steadfast love of the Lord never ceases, His mercies never come to an end; They are new every morning; Great is thy faithfulness. The Lord is my portion says my soul, therefore I will hope in him.

Many other stories in the bible demonstrate that the activating event (A) does not directly cause C. The stories often involve two different people who experience the same event, A, but who have different C's. For example, in Luke 10:38-42 it is said that Jesus went to visit the house of Martha and Mary. While Mary sat at the feet of Jesus and enjoyed his company, Martha ran around the house working. Eventually, Martha went to Jesus because she was troubled that her sister was not helping her. Jesus points out that Martha was troubling herself about many things and Mary had chosen the better part, which was not troubling at all. Martha was probably thinking thoughts such as, "Mary should be helping me with the work," "It isn't fair that she isn't helping," and "Jesus should tell her to help me."

Another example of the same activating event (A) being responded to with different C's is the story of Jesus coming upon the scene where an adulteress is about to be stoned for her sin. It is reasonable to assume that those who were about to stone her might have been thinking thoughts such as, "It is awful that she committed adultery, and she must be punished for it." Jesus, on the other hand, may have been thinking, "Adultery is a sin and certainly not good, but we have all sinned, so none of us has the right to punish a sinner. We can forgive and direct the sinner to refrain from future sin."

While the ABC emotional equation may be found at work within scripture, it doesn't necessarily follow that the Christian "way of seeing" would always agree with REBT's view that demandingness, awfulizing, LFT, and self-and other-downing are problematical.

Demandingness

The biblical view is that God alone is the creator and sustainer of the universe; consequently, God alone may legitimately demand. Humans on the other hand, although created in the image of God, are not God and have no legitimate authority to make absolute demands. Thus acting demandingly generally proves to be self-defeating and emotionally disturbing because our demands do not create reality in the way Christian theology says God's demands do. Thus, in the story of Jonah, Jonah, a mere mortal, is demanding that God punish the Ninevites. As a result, he makes himself enraged, which ultimately does not help him in any way.

Some individuals may claim that scripture tacitly approves of Christians being demanding about some issues. Such individuals might think that the Bible demands that we do the good and refrain from doing the bad. For example, a Christian should feed the poor but refrain from stealing. However, an important distinction needs to be made between "metaphysical demands" and "moral demands." A metaphysical demand is of the form, "Reality (R) must be a particular way," whereas a moral demand is of the form, "To be moral one must do or be Y." The moral demand can be written as a conditional (as an if-then statement), namely, "If one wants to be moral, then one should (must) do or be Y." Thus a moral demand is always a conditional, a non-absolute demand. A metaphysical demand, on the other hand, is never conditional; it is an absolute demand.

Let's consider some examples. If I am talking to Sam right now, then metaphysically I must be talking to him. I cannot be talking to him and not talking to him at the same time and under the same conditions. That would be a metaphysical impossibility. On the other hand, if I believe that as a Christian I should feed the poor, then what I am saying is that if I want to be a good Christian, then I should feed the poor. Feeding the poor is not a metaphysical demand because it is conceivable that someone doesn't care to be a good Christian, in which case there is no necessity to feed the poor. The moral demand is only binding if certain conditions are fulfilled, in this case, if I have the desire or wish to be a good Christian. However, if certain conditions have to be fulfilled for the moral demand to be binding, then it is not an absolute demand. In philosophical ethics the question is asked, "Why be moral?" There are many reasons offered for being moral, but the mere fact that reasons are given for why it is preferable to be moral demonstrates that morality is a choice, and because it is a choice, it is not a metaphysical demand or necessity.

I am aware that Kant held that moral demands are categorical or absolute. One statement of his categorical imperative is "I must act in such a way that I can at the same time will that my maxim of action be a universal law." Although Kant apparently believed that the categorical imperative is an absolute moral demand on a par with a metaphysical demand, the wording of the imperative reveals that it cannot be absolute in the metaphysical sense. If I have to will that my maxim of action be a universal law, then it is not a metaphysical absolute. Willing is irrelevant to a metaphysical absolute, and the fact that it is integral to acting morally demonstrates the contingent nature of the categorical imperative.

When God gives commandments (demands), as in the Decalogue, those are moral demands that are binding only if one wants to be moral, desires eternal life, etc. The Ten Commandments are not metaphysical demands; in other words, they do not create the reality they command. If they did, humans would have no choice but to honor parents, refrain from killing, avoid stealing and adultery, etc. The commandment "Thou shalt not kill" is contingent on one wanting to be moral and thus it would be better to state it in the following form: "If I want to be moral, then I must not kill." If "Thou shalt not kill" were truly a metaphysical "must" or demand, it would be impossible for humans to kill; but if you pick up any newspaper, you will see quite vividly that killing is not impossible. In fact, if moral demands were metaphysical demands, then humans would have no free will and morality would not make sense. Morality presupposes having the freedom to choose to act and to choose to refrain from acting.

REBT only declares as irrational and problematical the absolute metaphysical demands, not the conditional moral should's or ought's. In Christian terms, if God allows us the freedom to be moral or not moral, how can humans legitimately demand that others act as though they had no freedom and be the way we demand them to be?

Awfulizing

Anti-awfulizing is fundamentally scriptural. The biblical way of seeing is that nothing, absolutely nothing, can separate us from the love of God, and therefore, nothing is truly awful (Romans 8:39). Christian clients can also be directed to the following scriptural passages that are patently anti-awfulizing: Proverbs 3:25; Isaiah 41:10; Philippians 4:6-7; and Matthew 6:34.

Low Frustration Tolerance (LFT)

When REBT asserts that an event can never be truly awful, what is being said is that nothing is ever truly completely bad, as bad as it could possibly be, or world-shattering. It may be tragic, but never completely and utterly catastrophic in the sense of negating all meaning, purpose, and the possibility of future pleasure and happiness. This is not to be Pollyannaish or to make a mere semantic distinction. What is being asserted is that bad events do occur. If we are realistic, we will acknowledge the undesirability of the event, and perhaps even assert that we never want anyone to undergo such an event, but the event cannot metaphysically determine the future as utterly catastrophic. Why? Events simply are; they are metaphysical realities. Evaluations of events are mental acts. Evaluating an event as tragic, unfortunate, undesirable, or very painful is rational, because it is simply an evaluation about the event's current impact on oneself or others in light of one's life goals and values. Evaluating an event as awful, that is, utterly and completely devastating for all times and for all people, is irrational because a) it makes an absolute prediction about an unknown future, and b) it is an overgeneralization and exaggeration of the current data. Awfulizing implies that if the current situation is very unpleasant or tragic, the future must inevitably be so. It asserts the erroneous A → C relationship: Awfulizing says that because the current situation is very bad, I must feel very bad, and I will always feel that way because the event has negated the possibility of any future meaning, purpose, pleasure, or happiness in my life or anyone else's life.

Just as the biblical way of seeing is that there is nothing that is truly awful, then, correspondingly, there is nothing so bad we cannot stand it. Obviously, situations and circumstances can be unpleasant,very, very unpleasant, as we see in the story of Job,but because we are grounded and supported by the love of God, we can tolerate our lot. Numerous scriptural passages promote frustration tolerance. In his letter to the Philippians, St. Paul makes this point very strongly when he says, "For I have learned to find resources in myself whatever my circumstances," and "I have strength for anything through Him who give some power."

Low frustration tolerance can be insidious, and many Christians can succumb to it, while actually viewing their LFT as a virtue. This form of LFT is the assertion that "I am so weak and sinful, but God is so great; I can't do anything for myself, so, therefore, God must do it all for me." Job tries this tactic with God (Job 40:4-7). God's response to Job is instructive. Twice God tells Job to gird his loins, and that the questions of life will be posed by God to Job, not by Job to God. The work of finding the answers, however, is the work of Job and of all other humans. God makes it quite clear that it is the dignity of humans that we gird our loins, accept our majesty, and do the difficult work of finding answers to life's problems and alleviate the suffering that can be a part of life. We are not alone; God helps, but we are to do the work!

Endurance in the face of adversity and frustration is held up as a Christian ideal in scripture:

Indeed we call blessed those who showed endurance. You have heard of the endurance of Job, and you have seen the purpose of the Lord, how the Lord is compassionate and merciful. (James 5:11)

Self- and Other-Downing

Christians live with three fundamental theological realities:
+Everyone is created in the image of God.
+Everyone has sinned.
+Everyone can be redeemed by Christ.

The denial of any or all of these theological realities creates theological problems, and under certain circumstances may also create emotional problems.

Denial that everyone has sinned: To deny that humans sin, e.g., that they sometimes act in unloving or evil ways is a denial of reality. Evil exists in the world, and to deny it yields an overly-

Pollyannaish world view. By denying the reality of evil, people may put themselves in situations or in relationships that are dangerous or at least not in their best interests.

Denial that everyone is created in the image of God and can be redeemed by Christ: Few Christians would consciously deny such fundamental Christian beliefs, but they sometimes act as though they do. To deny that humans are created in the image of God and can be redeemed by Christ may lead some to view humans as merely sinners with no hope for being anything but a sinner perpetually enslaved to sin. The Christian view is that the Gospel or good news is that since we are created by God and have the possibility of being redeemed by Christ, we all have the potential to experience the great goodness of salvation. In Paul's letter to the Ephesians, he makes it clear that this salvation is an unmerited gift of God. It has nothing to do with something we have done; rather it is the result of the grace of God.

A Christian can only legitimately put herself, himself, or others down as utterly worthless or as total failures by embracing an irrational belief. St. Paul makes it clear that while we can accept that we are sinners, we are still worthwhile because we are loved by God, even in the midst of our sin. "But God proves his love for us in that while we still were sinners Christ died for us." (Romans 5:8). All humans are worthwhile because we are created and loved by God with the fullness of that love exemplified by Christ crucified. Human sin is real, but we can never legitimately reduce a human to sin. Thus the rational Christian accepts both that there is evil in the world and the potential for humans through the grace of God to transcend sin and to do the good. Kurt Vonnegut put it quite nicely, even if not with theological precision, in <u>Player Piano</u> when he wrote:

That there must be virtue in imperfection, for Man is imperfect, and Man is a creation of God,
That there must be virtual in frailty, for Man is frail, and
Man is a creation of God.

*That there must be virtue in inefficiency,
for Man is inefficient, and
Man is a creation of God.
That there must be virtue in brilliance
followed by stupidity, for Man is
alternatively brilliant and stupid, and
Man is a creation of God*

Even though scripture says, "For all have sinned and fall short of the glory of God," this belief does not mean that we should divisively down ourselves or others and thereby weaken the Christian community. The belief that Christians are members in the body of Christ can lead them to love and support each other, rather than put each other down.

Is REBT too Self-Centered?

In one study, Christian pastoral counselors were surveyed about their level of agreement or disagreement with what the authors took to be five principles of REBT. Those principles were:

+Irrational beliefs are the primary causes of feelings.
+People are limited and fallible.
+There is no valid way of evaluating the worth of people; hence there is no valid use for, or judge of, self-esteem.
+There are no pure "needs" or "musts" in life beyond our physical survival needs.
+People are best served when they function as long-range hedonists.

Over 75 per cent of those surveyed agreed with the first four principles, but 54 per cent disagreed with the fifth principle. One of the reasons people offered for disagreeing with this principle was that it appeared to them to encourage self-centeredness, whereas the Christian ideal is a balance of self and community (West and Reynolds 1997). But what does Albert Ellis actually mean by "long-range hedonism"? And is this phrase really inconsistent with Christian ideals? Ellis has written that his concept of "long-range hedonism" is not to be viewed as synonymous with Maslow's concept of "self-actualization," which has been criticized by some for being too individualistic, self-seeking, and indulgent. Ellis says that REBT includes both self-interest and social interest, and that individuals would be better served by being concerned about the welfare both of particular individuals and of one's community. In other words, REBT upholds both individualism and social involvement, and not just one to the exclusion of the other. In fact, Ellis has described the emotionally and mentally healthy individual as having the following traits:

>+Is considerate and fair to others
>+Avoids needlessly harming others
>+Engages in collaborative and cooperative endeavors
>+Is altruistic
>+Enjoys some measure of interpersonal and group relationships

Thus Ellis's concept of "long-range hedonism" is not synonymous with the overly-indulgent philosophy of "Eat, drink, and be merry, for tomorrow you may die." The latter is not only too short-ranged and indulgent, but also lacking in healthy self-interest. Ellis's concept is closer to the Christian ideal than it is to the overly self-interested ideal of Maslow's self-actualized individual.

It may be that it is the word "hedonism" to which some Christians are opposed. If "hedonism" connotes only pleasure seeking with an emphasis on the quantity of pleasure for the self rather than the quality of pleasure, then most Christians would likely oppose it. However, if we hold that there are qualitative differences among pleasures, then there may be less opposition. If pleasures such as doing the will of God, experiencing the joy of salvation, praising God, and loving our neighbor as ourselves are held to be qualitatively higher than the pleasure of eating a hamburger, buying a new pair of shoes, or getting an "A" on a calculus exam, then the word "pleasure" is less objectionable. Christians would not generally object to long-range hedonism as an ideal if that hedonism is understood it include and elevate the pleasure that comes from serving God and our neighbor and from being a child of God.

Special Problems Working with Christian Clients

Guilt: Many Christians live a considerable portion of their lives suffering from guilt. Many also believe that they should feel guilty; in fact, some Christians believe that scripture even seems to recommend and praise guilt. However, an important distinction needs to be made between remorse or godly grief and neurotic guilt and worldy grief.

Remorse, or godly grief, is the emotion people experience when they transgress what they take to be a rule of good behavior and wish that they had not done so. Although that feeling is unpleasant, it may spur one to repent and change one's ways to be more Christ-like.

Neurotic guilt, on the other hand, is the emotion people experience when they believe that they absolutely should not have transgressed a rule of good behavior and that they are no good or even worthless as a result. This form of guilt tends not to spur people to repent and change; rather, it leads to depression, inactivity, or a vicious cycle of beating themselves up emotionally, feeling guilty, tiring of the guilt, repeating the transgression, and beating up on themselves, *ad nauseum*.

When scripture talks about guilt, it is describing what REBT calls remorse or what St. Paul calls "godly grief."

I rejoice, not because you were grieved, but because you were grieved into repenting: for you felt a godly grief, so that you suffered no loss through us. For godly grief produces a repentance that leads to salvation and brings no regret, but worldy grief [guilt] produces death (II Corinthians 7:9-10)

What about the demand that seems to be a part of guilt? Some Christians believe that there are things that a Christian absolutely must not do. St. Paul makes it very clear that there is no such moral demand that has the force of a metaphysical demand.

Twice in his first letter to the Corinthians he says, "All things are lawful for me" (I Corinthians 6:12). He can do all things because he has free will. Once recognizing that fact, St. Paul could truly be moral because as he writes, "not all things are helpful." David Stoop, a Christian psychologist commenting on this passage says that the point is that "All things are lawful, so remove the demands on yourself" (1991, p. 122). Christians believe that Christ came to free people from slavery and condemnation, so why enslave oneself again with the demand behind guilt?

King David committed adultery and murder, but despite those sins he wrote, "[God] wash me thoroughly from my iniquity, and cleanse me from my sin." (Psalms 51:2-4). David assumes he is redeemable, and so he does not damn his entire self for his transgressions. He recognizes his deeds as wrong, and he asks for God's forgiveness. David concludes with, "Purge me with hyssop and I shall be clean; wash me, and I shall be whiter than snow." Focusing on God's grace that can restore him to purity, David avoids a self-deprecating guilt that offers no hope to be different. There is no self-blame or condemnation in him, but rather self-awareness, proper moral judgment of his actions, confession, and the acceptance of forgiveness and restoration.

You were dead through the trespasses and sins…But God who is rich in mercy, out of great love with which he loved us even when we were dead through our trespasses, made us alive together with Christ. (Ephesians 2:1, 4-5)

Bless the Lord, O my soul, and do not forget all his benefits-who forgives all your iniquity, who heals all your diseases, who redeems your life from the Pit, who crowns you with steadfast love and mercy, who satisfies you with good as long as you live so that your youth is renewed like the eagle's. (Psalms 103:2-5)

Unconditional Self Acceptance (USA) vs. Self-Rating

Closely related to guilt is self-rating. There would be no guilt unless a person rated herself or himself harshly. Many Christians believe that being a sinner demands self-rating. This makes it impossible, however, to accept oneself unconditionally.

For Christians, the greatest model of acceptance is God's acceptance of us in the act of salvation through Christ:

But when the goodness and loving-kindness of God our Savior appeared, He saved us, not because of any works of righteousness that we had done, but according to His mercy, through the water of rebirth and renewal by the Holy Spirit. (Titus 3:4-7)

Just as God was loving toward us and saved us without looking at our deeds or acts, but simply as an act of merciful acceptance on God's part, we too can lovingly accept ourselves and others regardless of our deeds. This does not mean that we accept or deny our sin and failings. Rather, it means that we will commit the godly act of evaluating our actions according to the norms of God, accept ourselves as God accepts us, and then cooperate with the Holy Spirit in doing the work necessary to change our behavior. This kind of unconditional self-acceptance is entirely consistent with Ellis's philosophy.

Suffering as Ordained by God: It is not uncommon for Christians who are undergoing some life crisis to say, "It is God's will." For some people this is an effective coping statement in the face of an unpleasant event. However, for others, especially those who hold the erroneous emotional equation, it can support the belief that their misery is inescapable, awful, and ordained be God. The obvious response to the latter is that although God may ordain the event (A), the free will of humans means that humans can choose their belief about the event, and consequently are responsible for their own misery. That is to say, God ordains A, but humans are responsible for B and C.

This response would not satisfy radically deterministic Christians, who hold that God determines not only the event (A), but B and C as well. They might hold that while psychologically one feels as though one has free will, in actuality that feeling is only an illusion and that it is God who absolutely determines everything. This view is scripturally problematic because while numerous biblical verses are commandments from God, what sense do moral commandments have unless there is some free will? Without free will a commandment is superfluous. Other verses, if not commandments, are directives from God; for example, "If today you hear his voice, harden not your heart." Again, what sense does such a verse make without free will? Thus it can be pointed out to clients that they choose to accept the deterministic belief that causes their misery.

Be Ye Therefore Perfect: Some Christians use the verse, "Be ye therefore perfect as your father who is in heaven is perfect" (Matthew 5:48) as a justification for self- or other-downing. Still other Christians accept the verse, but they don't torture themselves with it. How do the two groups differ? The individuals in the first group seem to demand that they must have all the attributes of God and be perfect. Clearly, if one accepts Anselm's definition of God as "that than which nothing greater can be conceived," then we are never perfect in that ontological sense. If Christians read the verse as command that humans are ontologically to fulfill the Anselmian definition, then God seems to be commanding impossibility, which would be unjust.

Matthew 5:48 is the last verse of the chapter, and it is the culmination of the entire chapter's discussion on loving action toward others, especially those who are difficult to love, such as one's enemies. The conclusion is that our perfection is in our love; however, this is at odds with what may be our natural tendency to love only our neighbor but not our enemy. The verse does not follow a discussion of the perfection of God, but rather how in the realm of human action loving forgiveness is a godly perfection and an ideal toward which Christians are to strive. Instead of ordering the impossible, it is acknowledging imperfection and directing Christians to accept this universal fact and to forgive others and oneself as God has forgiven us. "Be kind to one another, tender hearted, forgiving one another, as God in Christ has forgiven you." (Ephesians 4:32). Our perfection is our love and that love is perfection because God is love and desires love.

Religious Interventions within an REBT Framework

The general strategy of REBT is to help people dispute the irrational beliefs that cause dysfunctional negative emotions and self-defeating behaviors, and then replace them with rational beliefs. If a belief is a map and something by which we can steer, then at least two approaches may help us change an irrational belief. The direct and elegant approach would be to change the map, the irrational belief itself. This is the elegant solution, since once we are able to see more rightly or clearly, then steering through life becomes more proficient. However, sometimes people cling tenaciously to wild fanciful maps out of habit and fear of the unknown map, despite the pain and failures that the inadequate map causes them. When this kind of clinging is extremely tenacious, the psychotherapist might better expend energy by taking an indirect, inelegant approach by encouraging the client to steer differently for a while without directly attacking the irrational belief. This is not a new concept: AA advocates "fake it until you make it," in other words, act as if you believed and felt differently. Emerson said, "If you have not a virtue, assume it." More successful steering through life may loosen the grip on the irrational belief and help the individual adopt a more adequate one and ultimately feel and behave better.

Let us consider a client who has a phobia of riding in elevators. His irrational belief is "The elevator might malfunction and I might plunge to my death, and that would be horrible." Rather than having the client dispute the awfulizing or the overgeneralization, the therapist might encourage him to ride in elevators while practicing relaxation techniques. The relaxation techniques may decrease the client's level of anxiety, and while the client is dependent on the distraction, at least he may be able to ride in elevators. Of course, a more elegant solution would be to have the client replace the irrational beliefs behind the anxiety with rational ones that help him to be concerned about riding in elevators, but not overly-anxious.

How can religion be used as something more than mere distraction but rather to dispute an irrational belief and change the person's map? In the following section, I will offer several uses of religion within REBT that therapists may find helpful in working with Christian clients who are open to such interventions and desire interventions consistent with their faith.

Prayer: Most prayers acknowledge the adversity (A) and perhaps the pain and suffering of the individual (C), and then proceed to ask God either to change A to a more pleasant one or to grant the individual the ability to accept the suffering as part of God's plan. Ignored is the individual's contribution to C, namely, his or her irrational beliefs. The erroneous emotional equation is reinforced by such thinking as "A happens; I can't help but feel C, but the omnipotent God can either change A or C, and I will feel better either way."

I use an alternative form of prayer when working with some Christian clients for whom prayer is important and desirable. What the client is to do in the REBT-structured prayer is as follows:

+Early within the prayer acknowledge the A and C
+Name the irrational beliefs (demands plus derivatives)
+Name the corresponding rational beliefs
+Ask for God's help in achieving a more rational belief and a healthier negative emotion.
+Pray the prayer several times a day over an agreed upon time span

The REBT structured prayer is considerably different from the form used by most Christian psychotherapists and pastoral counselors, even those therapists/counselors who purport to embrace a CBT form of therapy. For example, Craigie and Tan (1989) write,

Indeed praying with clients that they may be liberated from resistant mis-beliefs, that they may be empowered to do the truth, and that they may come into a deeper relationship with the truth can sometimes be a most powerful experience.

Note that the form of prayer mentioned by Craigie and Tan has the therapist praying with the client for the client's liberation from irrational beliefs. However, in this form of prayer the client may be overly-passive. He or she may not be actively disputing his or her irrational beliefs within the context of the prayer. The passivity may reinforce the client's irrational belief in their helplessness and their low frustration tolerance; namely that disputing their irrational beliefs is too difficult, so let God and their therapist liberate them from that work. Wouldn't it be more helpful to have clients experience cooperatively working with God to dispute their irrational beliefs than having God or the therapist do it all?

I have the client compose the prayer in the therapy session; we then write it down, and I keep a copy in the client's file. The client also keeps a copy to pray several times a day between sessions. Sometimes I have them do only this kind of dispute; and at other times, it is done with the traditional disputes.

Some pastoral counselors have rightfully questioned the use of prayer in therapy. When prayer is a mere distraction, it should be used very cautiously and always with an eye toward eventually disputing the irrational beliefs directly. Where prayer takes the responsibility away from the client in pursuing change and fosters client dependency, it should be avoided in the therapy session. On the other hand, when the client experiences prayer as a partnership with the therapist and God, to have the client actively dispute the irrational beliefs can be effective. Always keep track of the effectiveness of this intervention.

I met with a 40-year-old single male, who had a cardiac condition that was beyond help. He was extremely anxious and afraid of his imminent death. In the hospital he was screaming and crying so loudly that it disrupted the other patients and the medical staff. Together we composed the following prayer that he said at least three times per day for the four weeks before his death:

Oh God, source of all goodness and wisdom, I am anxious and afraid about my death, which may come very soon, because I keep telling myself that it will be unbearable. Help me to remember your Holy Word in which you promise that You will neither let us be tested beyond our powers, nor face any trial beyond what we can bear. Let me not test myself or worry myself more than You would ask, nor make my very real burden unbearable. Help me to experience the Kingdom of God that is at hand in which you lovingly call me beyond my anxiety and past my fears into Your peace. Grant me the strength to be concerned about my fate so that I put my affairs in order for those I love, but to realize that in Your Kingdom nothing is unbearable because whatever happens, including my death, nothing can separate me from your love. I ask this through Jesus my brother, the Light and Life of the world. Amen.

A devout Christian for whom prayer was very important, he eventually accepted his condition and his impending death and was able to write letters to those he loved. By the third week, a week before his death, he went from room to room, with the help of a wheelchair, visiting other patients and helping to lift their spirits. He died very peacefully.

I saw another client who experienced severe depression for years. While we did not use prayer in session, during our last session I recommended that she form a prayer circle at her church in which she would teach REBT and use it in prayers within the prayer circle. She took up my suggestion and later reported back to me that she was experiencing it as very helpful for her and to many of the other women in the group.

I will go more in depth on the issue of prayer in the second part of this book. At that time I will go even more in depth on rational and irrational thoughts since this is so crucial to psychotherapeutically effective prayer. Some of it will seem like a review but it is essential that you grasp how to identify the irrational beliefs that can sneak into your client's prayer. I will also cover a number of sample prayers for various A's so that you can see how to incorporate the ABC into prayer.

Meditation: When pastoral counseling has employed meditation or guided imagery, the technique has generally functioned as a distraction, which interrupts the client's obsessively ruminating about the adversities in her or his life. While distraction can work to alleviate symptoms, it rarely gets at the irrational beliefs underlying the problem. Thus meditation or guided imagery as mere distraction is inelegant and necessitates continued meditation. Of course, there are worse activities than meditation; but the elegant solution would be to eradicate the irrational beliefs that form the basis of the rumination.

The following is a slight variation on REBT's technique of rational-emotive imagery (REI). In religious REI, the therapist has the client do the following:

+Image the problematical A
+Feel the unhealthy C
+Stop the meditation as soon as the unhealthy C is experienced
+Identify the irrational belief(s) contributing to the C
+Resume the meditation by imagining the problematical A again
+Call upon and/or imagine Jesus or God disputing the irrational belief so that the client feels a C that is a healthy alternative to the unhealthy C
+Identify the rational belief God and/or Jesus (and the client) would want the client to embrace.

+Practice the meditation at home or the office every day over an agreed upon time span

Scripture: Ellis wrote,

I think I can safely say that the Judeo-Christian Bible is a self-help book that has probably enabled more people to make more extensive and intensive personality and behavioral changes than all professional therapists combined. (336)

Several therapists, secular and religious, have used scripture in conjunction with REBT to dispute irrational beliefs. For example, Hank Robb's booklet, How to Stop Driving Yourself Crazy with Help from the Bible, lists common irrational beliefs and then identifies scriptural passages that seemingly refute or dispute the irrational beliefs [In the "Resources" section of this publication, you will find a reference to the Albert Ellis Institute from which you can order Dr. Robb's booklet.] This is probably the most common religious method employed in a religiously-oriented use of REBT.

This approach may be a very effective technique when working with conservative Christian clients who see scripture as the sole source of authority for their faith. The process is simple. Each of the client's irrational beliefs is paired with a scripture expressing a relevant rational belief. For example, if the person is awfulizing, then the therapist or client chooses the anti-awfulizing scriptural passage closest to the client's circumstance.

With Christians who are less conservative and may not take the Bible literally, the therapist or the client approach scripture differently. If the Christian client views scripture as myth (myth not as untrue story but as story functioning to reveal deep and significant aspects of human experience and Divine-human interaction that could not be captured by a newspaper or textbook approach to truth), then biblical stories can be used to demonstrate rational beliefs that help with difficult human conditions.

For example, liberal Christians may not believe there was an actual Jonah who was swallowed by an actual divinely appointed creature. They may instead see the story as revealing the all too common tendency to avoid unpleasant tasks, to be overly self-centered, lack trust, and to demand that lie and others be the way we want them to be, all of which create and intensify our misery and alienation from others, ourselves, and God. People do not have to believe in a historical suffering Job to see that crying "Why me: ain't it awful?" about one's misfortunes gets them nowhere but feeling even more miserable. However, people realize from the story that God tells Job that God asks the big questions of life, and it is Job's responsibility to come up with the answers to those big questions or live with the not knowing. What helps Job to assume that responsibility, which god says is a part of human dignity, is the realization that even in the midst of the misfortune God is with Job and God will always be with him.

Should the therapist engage in a duel with the client's irrational beliefs using relevant biblical verses or engage in selective story telling? The choice is best determined by finding out how the client views scripture. Let the client's attitude toward scripture be the guide.

The following is a list of scriptural passages that may be useful for disputes. The verses are categorized by the type of irrational belief they dispute.

Demandingness
+I must/must not do this thing:
All things are lawful unto me, but all things are not expedient: all things are lawful for me, but I will not be brought under the power of any. (I Corinthians 6:12)

+I must be loved:
If you find that the world hates you know that has hated me before you. If you belong to the world, it would love you as its own; the

reason it hates you is that you do not belong to the world. (John 15:18-19)

+I must be treated fairly. Life should be fair:
Anyone who wants to live a godly life in Christ Jesus can expect to be persecuted. (II Timothy 3:12)

+I must not suffer. Life should be free from suffering:
I tell you all this that in me you may find peace. You will suffer in the world. But take courage! I have overcome the world. (John 16:33)

Awfulizing
For I am persuaded, that neither death, nor life, nor angels, nor principalities, not powers, nor things present, nor things to come. Not height, nor depth, nor any other creature, shall be able to separate us from the love of God, which is in Christ Jesus our Lord.) (Romans 8:38-39)

Dismiss all anxiety from your minds. Present your needs to God in every form of prayer and in petitions full of gratitude. Then God's own peace, which is beyond all understanding, will stand guard over your hearts and minds, in Christ Jesus (Philippians 4:6-7)

Fear not. I am with you: Be not dismayed: I am your God. I will strengthen you, and help you and uphold you with my right hand of justice...for I am the Lord, your God, who grasps your right hand: It is I who say to you, "Fear not, I will help you." (Isaiah 4:10, 13)

Be not afraid of sudden terror, of the ruin of the wicked when it comes; for the Lord will be our confidence, and will keep your foot from the snare. (Proverbs 3:25-26)

Blest are those persecuted for holiness' sake; the reign of God is theirs. Blest are you when they insult you and persecute you and utter every kind of slander against you because of me. Be glad and rejoice, for your reward is great in heaven: They persecuted the prophets before you in the very same way. (Matthew 5:10-12)

I consider the sufferings of the present to be as nothing compared with the glory to be revealed in us. (Romans 8:18)

Peace is my farewell to you, my peace is my gift to you; I do not give it to you as the world gives peace. Do not be distressed or fearful. (John 14:27)

Which of you by worrying can add a moment to his life-span? (Matthew 6:27)

Come to me, all you who are weary and find life burdensome, and I will refresh you. Take my yoke upon your shoulders and learn from me, for I am gentle and humble of heart. Your souls will find rest, for my yoke is easy and my burden light. (Matthew 11:18-30)

You will hear of wars and rumors of wars. Do not be alarmed. Such things are bound to happen, but that is not yet the end. Nation will rise against nation, one kingdom against another. There will be famine and pestilence and earthquakes in many places. These are the early stages of the birth pangs. They will hand you over to torture and kill you. Indeed you will be hated by all nations on my account. Many will falter then, betraying and hating one another. False prophets will rise in great numbers to mislead many. Because of the increase of evil, the love of most will grow cold. The man who holds out to the end, however, is the one who will see salvation. (Matthew 24:6-13)

Low Frustration Tolerance

I give no thought to what lies ahead but push on to what is ahead. (Philippians 3:13)

I do not say this because I am in want, for whatever the situation I find myself in I have learned to be self-sufficient. (Philippians 4:11)

I am experienced in being brought low, yet I know what it is to have an abundance. I have learned how to cope with every circumstance—how to eat well or go hungry, to be well provided for or do without. In Him who is the source of my strength I have strength for everything. (Philippians 4:12-13)

I warn you then: Do not worry about your livelihood, what you are to eat or drink or use for clothing. Is not life more than food? Is not the body more valuable than clothes? (Matthew 6:25)

No test has been sent you that does not come to all men. Besides, God keeps his promise. He will not let you be tested beyond your strength. Along with the test He will give you a way out of it so that you may be able to endure it. (I Corinthians 10:13)

Our desire is that each of you shows the same zeal till the end, fully assured of that for which you hope. Do not grow lazy, but imitate those who, through faith and patience, are inheriting the promises. (Hebrews 6:11-12)

They [earthly fathers] disciplined us as seemed right to them, to prepare us for the short span of mortal life; but God does so for our true profit, that we may share His holiness. AT the time it is administered, all discipline seems a cause for grief and not for joy, but later it brings forth the fruit of peace and justice to those who are trained in its school. (Hebrews 12:10-11)

Blessed be God...the Father of mercies, and the God of all comfort; Who comforts us in all our tribulation, that we may be able to comfort them which are in any trouble, but the comfort wherewith we ourselves are comforted of God. (II Corinthians 1:3-4)

Self- and Other-Downing

But God commends his love toward us, in that, while we were yet sinners, Christ died for us. (Romans 5:8)

For all have sinned and come short of the glory of God. (Romans 3:23)

And, behold, one came and said unto Him [Jesus], Good Master, what good thing shall I do, that I may have eternal life? And He said unto him, Why call thou me good? There is none good but one, that is God: but if thou will enter into life, keep the commandments. (Matthew 19:16-17)

Be kind to one another, tender hearted, forgiving one another, as God in Christ has forgiven you. (Ephesians 4:32)

Ye have heard that it has been said, thou shall love they neighbor, and hate thine enemy. But I say unto you, Love your enemies, bless them that curse you, do good to them that hate you, and pray for them which despitefully use you, and persecute you. (Matthew 5:43-44)

Then came Peter to him, and said, Lord, how often shall my brother sin against me, and I forgive him? Till seven times? Jesus said unto him, I say not unto thee, until seven times; but, until seventy times seven. (Matthew 18:21-22)

Special Passages for Guilt and Forgiveness

I rejoice, not because you were grieved, but because you were grieved into repenting; for you felt a godly grief, so that you suffered no loss through us. For godly grief produces a repentance that leads to salvation and brings no regret, but worldly grief [guilt] produces death. (II Corinthians 7:9-10)

You were dead through the trespasses and sins...but God Who is rich in mercy, out of great love with which He loved us even when we were dead through our trespasses, made us alive together with Christ. (Ephesians 2:1, 4-5)

Bless the Lord, O my soul, and do not forget all His benefits-Who forgives all your iniquity, Who heals all your diseases, Who redeems your life from the Pit, Who crowns you with steadfast love and mercy, Who satisfies you with good as long as you love so that your youth is renewed like the eagle's. (Psalms 103:2-5)

But when the goodness and lovingkindness of God our Savior appeared, He saved us, not because of any works of righteousness that we had done, but according to His mercy, through the water of rebirth and renewal by the Holy Spirit. (Titus 3:4-7)

Purge me with hyssop and I shall be clean; wash me and I shall be whiter than snow. (Psalms 51:7)

Confession to God: It is not surprising that the pastoral counseling movement began within mainline Protestantism rather than Roman Catholicism or Eastern Orthodoxy. The latter two had the confessional in which the penitent sought psychological relief from the guilt associated with sinning. While many Protestants may not be comfortable with a highly formalized rite of reconciliation, a less ritualized rite may be helpful for some Christians to overcome the self-downing that is a part of guilt. In REBT terms, a confessional or reconciliation ritual can function as an attack on people's shame of failing or sinning, and on their self-downing, and can even be a declaration that they can transcend the sin-that the sin is not one's fate.

I frequently have clients compose their own rite of reconciliation or a forgiveness ritual (what Mitchell Robin calls "Rites for Wrongs") that can be performed alone or with a group. I give the clients the freedom to incorporate whatever elements they find meaningful, with the following directives:

> +Acknowledge at some point early in the ritual the feeling of guilt or shame.
> +Distinguish between godly grief and neurotic guilt or shame and ask God's help to achieve godly grief.
> +If there is neurotic guilt or shame, identify the irrational beliefs behind it-the self-downing and awfulizing.
> +Praise God for the advantages of godly grief over neurotic guilt or shame (include a litany of advantages.
> +Pronounce your acceptance of God's love and forgiveness and your ability to tolerate the unpleasantness of the godly grief.
> +Try to sin that sin no more
> +Think of ways to help you avoid sinning in that way.
> +Ask for God's help to avoid the sin.

Fasting: REBT describes two types of anxiety: discomfort anxiety and ego anxiety. Behind discomfort anxiety is frequently low frustration tolerance, the belief that "I can't stand the discomfort." Most people with low frustration tolerance try to avoid the activating event or adversity associated with the discomfort. To help clients develop high frustration tolerance, the therapist guides them in disputing the low frustration tolerance and encourages them to embrace frustrating situations and develop the courage to withstand the frustration.

The practice of fasting may be a way to help some Christian clients develop high frustration tolerance. For Christian clients for whom fasting is meaningful (and medically permissible) I have them engage in an REBT form of fasting that has the following elements:

+The client is asked to notice any discomfort during the fasting, especially a desire to break the fast early.
+The client identifies the irrational beliefs behind the actual or imagined efforts to sabotage the fast or associated with great frustration.
+The client visualizes Jesus or God offering a rational belief, such as, "This isn't pleasant, but you can handle it. I am with you always." If a client does not believe that it is theologically permissible to visualize Jesus, then they can use their own words or choose words from scripture.
+The client repeats the rational belief forcefully and repeatedly.
+The client thanks God for giving her or him the strength to handle the frustration.

I have clients who use fasting as an occasion to tackle other areas of low frustration tolerance, for example, the low frustration tolerance associated with working with unpleasant coworkers. Handling the fast is a reminder that the client can handle almost any frustration that is nothing more than a frustration.

Religious Self-Talk: Many Christians frequently repeat to themselves short irrational phrases such as, "I'm no good," "That's awful," "I can't stand it anymore," and "I am nothing but a miserable sinner." For centuries the Roman Catholic Church has had very short prayers or utterances to help individuals maintain a religious consciousness and uplift themselves. Having Christian clients frequently repeat phrases such as the following can help the client replace the irrational phrases with more functional ones:

+I'm a person who occasionally sins, not a person who only sins.

+Oh happy sin (fault) that I should receive such a Redeemer.
+I am loved by God even when I act unlovingly.
+God doesn't create failures, only people who sometimes fail.
+God gives us hassles for character, never horrors to destroy us.
+I am loved simply because I am.
+Nothing can separate me from the love of God-absolutely nothing or no one!
+Hate the sin; love the sinner.

"Christian Hope Chest": One of the most problematical and most recurrent emotions for Christian is guilt. Frequently, Christians create guilt because they see themselves as transgressing a law or the love of God, they irrationally equate their being with their doing, and then they down themselves for the bad action. I have developed a technique to move the Christian from focusing on the sin and self-downing to embrace hope. One of my clients called the technique "The Christian Hope Chest."

The technique is simple. On a piece of paper the client creates three columns. One column is headed "Sinful Act," another is headed "Undesired Consequences," and the third column is headed "God's Grace." Under the first column, the client describes the act seen as a sin or sinful. Next to it in the second column, the client lists the undesirable consequences of the sinful act, both actual and possible. In the final column, she or he lists ways in which God could help the person move beyond the undesirable consequences and experience grace.

The Christian client through this technique realistically acknowledges the undesirable consequences of her or his actions, but has mobilized religious resources to move beyond the self-downing and awfulizing about those unpleasant consequences. In this way we can help the client move from anxiety, guilt, or depression to remorse, self-acceptance, and hope.

Witnessing as Shame Attack: Ellis was famous for the "shame attacks" he prescribed for clients and those who attended his REBT training programs. A shame attack is an exercise in which one does something that she or he would normally experience as shameful or embarrassing. For example, one could ride on the subway and yell the name of the stops wherever the train stops. An adaptation of the technique for Christians is to have the ashamed person talk to a stranger or colleague about their Christian faith and what it means to them. For those Christians who would not experience this as shameful or embarrassing, the technique may not be beneficial. However, for those who are embarrassed about sharing their faith or who tend to hide it, the technique, if practiced, may help the person identify the irrational beliefs beneath the shame and embarrassment that prevent them from witnessing. It can also be a way to help clients with social anxiety learn some social skills to talk to people about sensitive issues.

Prayer in More Depth

We prayed to our God and posted a guard day and night to meet this threat—Nehemiah 4:9

Introduction

Prayer is tremendously important to a life of ultimate meaning and purpose. It can also help you during periods of stress or crisis. Numerous studies have demonstrated that good mental health and a sense of well-being are also associated with faith put into action. Clearly, having faith in action is related to a number of important benefits. These benefits are maximized when we view ourselves as actively partnering with a loving God. On the other hand, few benefits occur if one adopts a passive stance and hopes that God will do it all for them.

What is a passive stance with respect to prayer, or passive prayer? It is treating prayer as a way merely to present to God those things you want God to do? When you pray, do you ask God to do everything for you while you passively sit back and wait for the wonderful miracles to take place? If so, that is passive prayer. Most of us, even if we are "go-getters" in most of our life, far too often become overly-passive creatures in our prayer life.

Passive prayer isn't horrible—something to avoid all the time. It is certainly better than not praying, and it is just fine and good to present to God our desires (Philippians 4:6-7). However, it can be a sign of spiritual immaturity if the bulk of our prayer is asking God to do everything for us without us taking responsibility for cooperating with God's grace through our actions and effort. I contend that when passive prayer makes up the bulk of our prayer life, it robs us of many potential benefits. In fact, it can even under certain circumstances actually reinforce or intensify our problems—mental, emotional, behavioral, and spiritual. For example, let's say that John is depressed after the breakup of an important relationship. In John's prayer to God, he might say something such as,

"I am so depressed God. I have broken up with Mary and I just can't stand the hurt. Please change her heart so she loves me again and take away the hurt I am feeling."

Notice that in the prayer, John portrays himself as weak and unable to stand the feelings he is experiencing. Moreover, rather than partnering with God to see whether he can change his behavior and see whether Mary's feelings toward him change, he asks God to do it all—to change Mary's heart and to remove his hurt. This is a classic example of a passive prayer which if overdone could result in the person feeling stuck in a well of passivity and helplessness. Even if God chose to change Mary's heart and remove John's hurt, John would not have learned how to have patience, tolerate a difficult situation, and consider his own contribution to his misery. Sometimes God does answer a passive prayer in the way we would like because God knows that would be in our best interests. However, God also wants us to mature spiritually and partner with Him rather than be overly-passive.

Have you ever paid really close attention to how people pray? How aware are you about how you pray? I surveyed approximately 3,000 prayers posted on the internet to determine what people pray about. The results of the survey were both enlightening and astounding. Since taking the survey, I have paid attention to the prayer requests of attendees at a single church in the Northeast. What I have found in the church is in substantial agreement with the findings of the survey, which can be summarized as follows:

+ People tend to pray passively rather than actively.
+ People tend to pray for two things:
++ For God to change their life situation (or people in those situations)
++ For God to change the their emotions and/or behaviors

Notice that these prayers have God doing and us receiving. This short book is about us praying such that God is doing and we are receiving **and** doing with Him. This is dynamic prayer. The book is meant to be read actively, not passively. Don't merely sit and read it from cover to cover. Read and practice; read and do! Rather than just praying about life situations, emotions, and behaviors, we will focus also on asking God to help us change our thoughts. In a few minutes you will see why it is so important to change the way you think and why it would be a good idea to pray about that kind of deep change within yourself. You will learn how to construct a prayer of your own that asks for transformation within you as much as a change outside you.

After you have learned this form of praying and tried it, I want you to do one simple thing. Ask yourself the following question: If I received the very thing for which I prayed, how would my life be different—concretely or visibly different? List 3-5 ways in which your life would be visibly different. For example, if John prays that he cooperate with God so that his depression is lifted, he might identify the following as things that would be concretely different in his life if his depression lifted:

+ He might get out of bed at 7 am each morning
+ He would eat a nutritionally balanced breakfast
+ He would exercise for 30 minutes daily
+ He would volunteer to help at church

God will do God's part of keeping the deal to help John lift his depression, but John's part of the deal is to do the things that God helped him identify as signs that his depression has lifted. So…John would get out of bed by 7 am. He would eat a balanced breakfast. He would exercise 30 minutes each day. He would volunteer in the church. After doing each of these things, he would praise God for creating him such that he can be a partner with God and enjoy the benefits of life.

It is important that the 3-5 items you list be very specific rather than vague. Notice that John said that he would exercise 30 minutes each day instead of saying that he would live a healthy lifestyle. Living a healthy lifestyle is simply too vague. What does a healthy life style look like? Every item on your list should be something that someone could see if they were to look at you in action. What would they see you doing?

Remember that even if you pray the type of active prayers described in this booklet, God will answer prayers in God's time and in God's way. This is the wisdom of God. He wants us to learn patience, persistence, and trust. Prayer is not magic, nor is it a tool to coerce God into doing what we think He ought to do. People who pray this kind of coercive prayer usually end up being angry with God that He did follow their demand not so subtly hidden within their coercive prayer. Frankly, I don't think that a coercive prayer is actually a prayer. It is a mere demand that we place on God and we really have no right to be demanding that God do what we want Him to do. Prayer is laying our concerns before God in a way that would have us grow spiritually. Demandingness toward God is not a trait of spiritual maturity, but a trait of spiritual immaturity.

Watch your thinking. Dynamic prayer is about changing what we believe. What we believe and the focus of our thoughts and prayers make all the difference in the world. One very clear example from scripture about the importance of our thoughts is in the third chapter of the book of Lamentations. In the first 19 verses we get the picture of a very depressed and anxious Jeremiah. He describes himself as the man who has seen affliction and who is now driven into darkness without light. He feels as though he is wasting away and is enveloped in bitterness. The world seems to wall him in and there are heavy chains upon him as he cries out, seemingly with no answer from God. God actually seems to him like a bear or a lion ready to pounce on him, tear him apart, leaving him desolate. He is without any sense of peace and is utterly without happiness. Then we get the powerful verse that reveals why Jeremiah feels so miserable. Verse 20 says that Jeremiah dwells on these thoughts day and night—not just once or twice, but continually, day and night.

Finally, Jeremiah changes the focus of his thinking. In verse 21 it says that he calls to mind the truth. The steadfast love of the Lord never ceases. God's mercies and blessings are new every morning and they never come to an end. Jeremiah shifts his focus to the goodness of the Lord. When Jeremiah's thinking changes, he moves from depression to hope. One can witness in these verses how the prayers of Jeremiah changed from asking the Lord to deliver him from the depression and the negative situations of life, to the goodness of the Lord and asking God's help to see his life situation rightly. His thinking shifted from passive thoughts of being a puppet of the negative situations of life to dynamic thoughts where he is a partner with God seeing life as filled with hope and wonderful possibilities and realities.

Frequently we are plagued with thoughts and beliefs that sabotage us in our prayer and in our spiritual growth. Albert Ellis, the famous psychologist, although not a Christian, praised the Bible for being the best self-help book ever written. In fact, he wrote that it helped more people over a longer period of time than all the psychologists, support groups, and psychological theories combined. I knew Dr. Ellis personally, and thank God for my relationship with him because he developed a theory about the important relationships among our thoughts, behaviors, and emotions. It is amazing how his theory is in agreement with what the Bible revealed more than 3,000 years ago. Dr. Ellis helped us realize that usually lurking beneath our unhealthy emotions and self-sabotaging behaviors there is a demand, an ungodly demand. Some examples of sabotaging thoughts are as follows:

+ I *need* this prayer answered immediately.
+ This situation *must* change or I will be miserable.
+ God *should* answer my prayers in the way I want them answered.
+ During my difficult time, the Christian community *ought* to support me in the way I want to be supported.
+ I *have to* be free from this concern before I can experience any purpose, meaning, or happiness.
+ I am a Christian, so I *shouldn't* be dealing with this kind of a problem anymore.

+ My spouse and I *should* be on the same page about important matters.

These ungodly thoughts often find their way into our prayers and thereby rob prayer of its power.

Invariably, an individual will say that when she/he prays passively, she/he feels better. That may be true. However, there is a big difference between *feeling better* and *getting better*. We live in an age when feelings are deified, and so we erroneously think that the ultimate goal is to feel better even if we make absolutely no change in our life, no change in our attitudes, desires, behaviors, and emotions. The goal of active prayer is to *get better and grow spiritually*, not just feel better. **That is my prayer for you—that you get better and glorify God through your emotions, thoughts, and actions rather than just feel better in the moment.** I want you to make lasting changes in your life. Think what a powerful witness it would be if you cooperated with God and through your prayer life you actually made important visible changes in your life. No one can argue against an actual transformation in your life. Think about what a witness you would have you made changes such as the following:

+ Your marriage improved.
+ You had better relationships with your co-workers, including your boss.
+ You lost weight, began exercising, and got control over some of your health conditions.
+ You looked happier—smiled more, encouraged others….
+ You helped people in need in very concrete and loving ways.

The Parts of a Dynamic Prayer

Scripture says in Proverbs, "For as a man thinks in his heart, so is he." This means that over and above our inherited biological tendencies, we frequently disturb our self by the kind of thoughts we have. Albert Ellis has given us a simple model for putting into

practice for our benefit this scriptural insight. If you know the alphabet to the letter "D", you can construct a dynamic prayer. Let's first list what each letter stands for and then practice writing a dynamic prayer:

> Let "A" = an **adversity** of life—something negative from your past, present, or anticipated in the future
> Let "B" = **beliefs**—your thoughts
> Let "C" = **consequences**—your emotions, behaviors, or physical symptoms
> Let "D" = your **disputes** or arguments against your unhelpful or ungodly beliefs

Adversity: An adversity is anything that happens in life that we consider to be a negative. Our beliefs are those thoughts that we have about the adversity. Some of the beliefs can be helpful and others are unhelpful. Helpful beliefs help us achieve our godly goals and cause emotions that are not deeply painful but negative enough that they spur us to make the necessary changes to achieve those goals. Unhelpful beliefs are very painful and tend to sabotage us from reaching our godly goals.

Consequences: Consequences are emotions, behaviors, and physiological responses that can either be helpful or unhelpful. We will not be covering physiological responses in this book.

Emotional consequences: Unhelpful emotions are those that sabotage us in reaching our goals or are intensely painful. The typical unhelpful emotions are:

+ Depression
+ Anxiety
+ Rage
+ Hurt
+ Guilt/shame
+ High frustration
+ Morbid jealousy

The typical helpful emotions are:
- Sadness
- Concern
- Annoyance
- Remorse
- Low frustration

Behavioral Consequences: Some of the more common unhelpful behaviors are:
- Procrastination
- Drinking/taking drugs
- Yelling, aggressive arguing
- Blaming
- Sulking
- Overeating
- Name-calling
- Avoiding
- Fighting
- Looking at pornography
- Being passive
- Whining
- Engaging in compulsive behaviors
- Cutting yourself, head banging, or other forms of self-injury

Unhelpful emotions and behaviors are largely caused by unhelpful beliefs and helpful emotions and behaviors are largely caused by helpful beliefs.

Beliefs: Unhelpful beliefs include the following:
- Demandingness
- Awfulizing
- Inadequate frustration tolerance
- Self-downing and, other-downing
- Overgeneralization

Demandingness is a form of unhelpful belief that usually contains words such as "should," "ought," "must," "have to," or "need." Examples of demandingness are:
+ I must be loved by the person I desire.
+ Christians ought to be hopeful at all times.
+ Life must be fair and free from hassles
+ You have to acknowledge all that I do for you.
+ I need to get a raise at my job.
+ I must be cured of this cancer.
+ God should answer my prayers in the exact way I want them answered by Him.

Demandingness is unhelpful because the world frequently fails to correspond to our demands and then we tend to disturb our self about the unfulfilled demand.

Awfulizing is a form of unhelpful belief that has the form "this event or situation is terrible, horrible, or awful." An example would be "It is awful when my children do not do what I ask them to do." Awfulizing is unhelpful because we are declaring that a situation negates all meaning, purpose, or future happiness when the reality is that a situation is only awful because we believe it to be awful. If we didn't awfulize, then the situation wouldn't be seen or experienced as awful. In other words, in our mind we make a situation awful; the situation in and of itself isn't awful. This doesn't mean that situations aren't bad; they often are. Sometimes they are very bad, even regrettably tragic, and it makes perfect sense not to want the situation to occur. However, awfulizing is a prediction about life in the future (declaring it to be void of meaning, purpose, etc.) Awfulizing fails to take into account the grace of God that can change situations or our ability to deal with them.

Another word for **inadequate frustration tolerance** is "I can't stand it-itis." When we believe that we can't stand a situation, then we feel very bad. This is unhelpful because the belief doesn't correspond to reality. Actually, there is usually considerable evidence that we can stand a situation. For example, I might hold the unhelpful belief that I can't stand it when Christians don't act lovingly. However, I have indeed encountered unloving Christians several times in my life and I am still alive. Obviously, I have stood it.

Self-downing is the belief that I am no good, a failure, useless, hopeless, or beyond redemption. This belief is unhelpful because it usually causes us to feel depressed or hopeless. It is also unhelpful because it doesn't correspond to reality. Self-downing is when we select some bad fact about our self and then generalize it to conclude that since it is bad, our entire self is bad. This is insidious spiritually because it negates the reality that we are created in the image of God. Of course, we are fallen and do bad things, but those bad things are never enough to negate the image of God that is a part of us. The same can be said for **other-downing**, which is holding the belief that others are no good, failures, useless, hopeless, or beyond redemption.

Overgeneralization is an unhelpful form of belief that I call false prophesy. This form of unhelpful belief usually contains the words "always," or "never." For example, "Mary will always reject my friendship," or "I will never have a fulfilling marriage." When we overgeneralize we are taking a current negative situation and projecting that situation and its negativity into the future. The reality is, however, that we have no privileged access to the future, so we can't legitimately assume we know what the future will bring. Why not trust in the power of God's grace and hope that He can help us have a meaningful future.

Helpful Beliefs: One of our goals is to transform our unhelpful beliefs into helpful ones. Consider the following:

+ **Helpful alternative to demandingness:** Instead of demandingness, we would embrace godly desires, hopes, wishes, and wants. Example: Instead of "I must do well on this exam," we would believe, "I hope I do well on this exam."

+ **Helpful alternative to awfulizing:** Instead of awfulizing, we would accept that a situation is negative without overly-exaggerating that negativity and seeing it as worse as the world could get. Example: Instead of "It would be awful if I got fired," we would believe, "It definitely would not be good to get fired, but it is not utterly devastating such that the world and my life now have no meaning, purpose, or conceivably good future."

+ **Helpful alternative to inadequate frustration tolerance:** Instead of having inadequate frustration tolerance, we would acknowledge that we don't like going through a particular situation, but realize that we can tolerate it. Example: Instead of "I can't stand it when the church plays praise music rather than hymns," we would believe "I really dislike praise music, but I can tolerate it. It isn't going to kill me."

+ **Helpful alternative to overgeneralization:** Instead of overgeneralizing, we would move away from such a black/white world view in which we think we absolutely know the future to one in which the future is open and all things are possible through the grace of God. Example: Instead of "These idiots in Washington, D.C. will never get anything good done," we would believe, "These people in Washington, D.C. are making a number of bad decisions, but I can pray that all of us, them included take more responsibility for the welfare of this country."

Dispute: A dispute is when we argue against an unhelpful belief and adopt a more helpful one. For example, instead of believing "I must be approved of by those who I deem important to me," which is a form of demandingness, I can dispute it. The dispute might take the form, "How is it helping me right now to hold this belief?" "Where is the evidence that I must be approved of by those individuals?" [Read II Timothy 3:12]. "How does it logically follow that because I would like to be approved of by those individuals that they must approve of me?" Notice that holding an unhelpful belief is never helpful, there is no evidence in support of it, and it simply isn't logical or theologically correct. We then adopt a more helpful belief such as, "I would like to be approved of by those who I deem important to me, but I don't need their approval, and if I don't get it, I might be sad about it, but I won't be devastated."

Notice that disputes can take three forms: pragmatic, empirical, and logical.

> **Pragmatic**: How is holding this unhelpful belief helping me?
> **Empirical**: Is there really any evidence supporting the unhelpful belief?
> **Logical**: How does it logically follow that because I want something that it must happen?

Let's see how disputing an unhelpful or ungodly belief is done. If Sandra believed, "It is awful when I walk into a church and people are not inviting," she could offer a pragmatic dispute against that belief by asking herself, "How is it helping me when I hold this belief? Does it help me feel closer to God, to fellow believers, or does it just have me want to leave the church and miss an opportunity to praise God in a community of believers?" She could also dispute her unhelpful belief by using an empirical dispute. An example of an empirical dispute she could use is, "Is there any evidence whatsoever that walking into a church of people who are not very inviting is so awful that it negates my meaning, purpose, and future happiness? I don't like it when people are uninviting, but is it truly as awful as having an inoperable brain tumor or war breaking out in the country?" Finally, an example of a logical dispute is, "Sure, I don't like walking into an uninviting church, but how does it logically follow that because I don't like it that it is truly awful? I am just having an exaggerated belief that isn't very helpful at all."

Composing a Dynamic Prayer

We now have all the building blocks to construct a dynamic prayer. Let's list the steps and then build an actual dynamic prayer.

Step 1: Briefly describe the adversity in your life

Step 2: Describe your negative emotions and behaviors; don't hide the negative stuff

Step 3: Be honest before God and list the unhelpful or ungodly thoughts and beliefs that you are holding about the adversity in your life

Step 4: Dispute or argue against the unhelpful and ungodly beliefs that you are holding. It is especially helpful to appeal to scripture and even quote it as you dispute your beliefs. [At the end of the book, I will list scriptural verses grouped as disputes of unhelpful/ungodly beliefs. Consider incorporating them into your prayer.]

Step 5: List the helpful and godly beliefs that you want God to help you adopt about your adversity in life

Sample Dynamic Prayer

Heavenly Father,

*I just lost my job **[Step 1]** and I am feeling very anxious and angry **[Step 2]** because I believe that I can't stand the thought that I might not be able to provide for my family and I believe my boss is a jerk who had no right to fire me **[Step 3]**. If I am truthful, I know that holding these beliefs isn't helpful to me; in fact, they just cause me to feel anxious and angry a good deal of the time, and I could better use my time in a job search and developing a budget to use at home rather than wallow in my anxiety and anger. In reality I can stand this unfortunate situation because you are with me and won't desert me. Most likely I will be able to find a new job with your help, one that will glorify You. Also, while I might not like what my boss did, that doesn't make him an evil individual. He was as much created in the image of God as I am, so he is a valuable human in his own right because you created him to be valuable **[Steps 4 & 5]**. Please help me to hold on to the helpful godly beliefs during this time so I don't get anxious and angry. Thank you for always being there to hear my prayer. It is a comfort knowing that in your holy word you say that nothing can separate me from your love, not even losing this job. Give me* *the strength to focus more on the mercies and blessings in my life more than on the current negative event. I bring this all before you in the precious name of Jesus. Amen.*

Let us say that Jonathan has just prayed the sample dynamic prayer. He would continue to pray this prayer daily until the anxious and angry spirit had passed. He would also think of 3-5 things he would do if he were no longer anxious and angry. For example, he might come up with the following list:

+ I will not worry more than 15 minutes per day about losing the job.
+ I will spend at least 6 hours per day making calls and networking to find a new job.
+ I will contact my boss to see whether he could be a good reference in my job search.

Jonathan would then do these three things in addition to praying.

In the following pages you will find prayers for specific situations and different states of your spirit. In addition to the dynamic prayers you construct and pray, you might also find helpful praying the following prayers. Remember, always act upon your prayer as if the prayer has already been answered and you were in a better place spiritually. Remember too that God is a loving God and has chosen to love you with your faults.

Using This Form of Prayer in the Church

This form of prayer can be so helpful in transforming emotions and behaviors that I have developed prayer groups within the church that use this prayer form. The group is usually made up of 5-8 individuals who bring their prayer issues to the group. Together they briefly discuss the issues within their lives without giving advice—just listening and supporting each other. When everyone has had some time to share their prayer issue, their emotions, and their behaviors, the group then shifts to praying for each other using the prayer form in this book. It is usually a good idea to have someone be the timekeeper and estimate how much time each person can take to make sure that everyone has time to be prayed for. It is usually a good idea to open the next prayer group meeting checking in with everyone covering the following:

> How each person is doing with respect to their adversity
> How their beliefs about the adversity have changed since the last meeting
> In what ways would each person like to grow spiritually regarding their particular adversity
> What each person has learned as a result of going through this adversity

In the following section, I have created prayers about specific adverse situations and troublesome behaviors and emotions. You can pray them just as they are written, but my hope is that you will view them as examples of dynamic prayers, models you could use to construct your own prayers in your own words. Don't get too hung up on "doing it perfectly." Remember, we want to confess our failings; resolve to change our thinking, behaviors, and emotions; and then cooperate with God's grace and work to make changes in our life so our deeply painful emotions are healed and we reach our spiritual goals. Ultimately the change within us is to glorify God and make His love and grace visible to a world desperately in need of Him.

Prayer for Overcoming Anxious Spirit

Lord,

All day I was thinking "what if," "what if," "what if." I worried that the situation I fear the most will be the very thing to happen—and that I won't be able to stand it. The anxiety wells up in me at times nearly to the point of panic. I feel as though it is eating me alive from the inside out.
Lord, give me the strength to hold captive those "what if's" and with your grace transform my "what if's" to "so what if's." Help me to say to myself, "so what if it does happen, then I can rely on my Lord to help me survive this as I have survived everything else in life through His grace."

Instead of dwelling on what I declare to be awful, I will remember to read Philippians 4:8 and then dwell on the positives you have placed in my life and will place in my future.

You do not want me to have a spirit of fear but of trust and assurance. I do trust you Lord because I have seen what You have done through Your Son to rescue us from lives without hope. I have seen how faithful you have been to believers throughout the ages. As always, Lord, I ask all this through Your Son, Jesus Christ.

Amen.

Prayer for an Overcoming an Angry Spirit

Heavenly Father,

I am boiling inside with anger because I keep telling myself that this situation I am going through is utterly intolerable and unbearable, and I dwell on how justified I am to be feeling this way. If I am honest with myself, I realize that these thoughts don't really help anything; they only make me hold on to my anger. It would be more helpful for me to listen to You when You inspired Paul to say, "Your anger does not bring about the righteous life that God desires." Clearly, you do not want me to stay so angry, but you know that at times I will, so you direct me in Your Holy Word, to place time limits on my anger rather than let it prolong. You also instruct me that if I make myself feel angry, that I am to refrain from acting on that anger.

Lord, I know that anger can destroy health and relationships. You have told us our body is a temple and that we are to love others as we love our self—not to destroy our self, our relationships, and hurt others. Help cleanse my temple, my body, of the anger that does not glorify you.

Please, Lord, help stop dwelling on how justified I am to be angry, and instead to focus on how unhelpful it is. Even better, let me shift my focus to what I need to do to live a righteous life rather than fooling myself that I am so perfect that I only experience righteous anger. Let my self-deception stop. Let me love instead of rage and thereby show the light of Christ through my life.

I ask this through the precious name of Jesus.

Amen

Prayer for Overcoming a Guilty Spirit

Heavenly Father,

We Christians, me included, are often very silly about guilt, partly because we confuse <u>being</u> guilty and <u>feeling</u> guilt. We think that when we are guilty, we should feel guilt. Rarely do we realize that You call us to repent and feel remorse rather than endlessly beating our self up and feeling guilt.

You have told us that godly grief, or remorse, leads to repentance that ends in salvation; whereas wordly grief, or guilt, ends in death—spiritual death.
Help me not to become so fixated on myself and my sin that I lose hope. Help me instead to focus on You and Your transforming grace. I don't want to take You for granted, so I acknowledge my sin, but I choose to love You and focus on my repentance and Your forgiveness rather than on the sin. I know and trust in my heart that the power of your forgiveness is greater than my guilt.

Let King David as we see in Psalm 51 be my mode because in that beautiful psalm we see so clearly how he allowed himself to be washed of his sin so he could become whiter than snow. I too want to be washed whiter than snow, so I accept Your forgiveness and ask Your help to avoid future sin.

I ask all this in the invaluable name of Jesus.

Amen

Prayer for Transcending Spiritual Dryness

Heavenly Father,

I try to pray, but I can't find any words right now. I read scripture, but I don't feel anything when I read it. I am in a period of spiritual desolation and I miss Your calming and uplifting presence. As it reads in Psalm 84, "My heart cries out for the living God."

Lord, I realize, however, that I live in an age that worships feelings, so I know I place too much value on having an emotional experience of You. The truth is—You are here even when I don't feel You. You love me, even when I don't feel Your love. Your greatness is beyond anything I can feel. Help me to trust that when I am in the midst of my emotional desert.

Let me enjoy the feeling of Your presence and Your love in your time. But...let me not become a slave to feeling good and end up worshipping the feeling of Your presence over the reality of You.

Let me realize that this may be a time when I love You with my mind and strength. Another day, I will love You with my emotions, and on that day I will enjoy the feeling of your presence that you will so graciously permit me to experience.

Help me to learn from this period of spiritual dryness how I completely and totally depend on you for everything.

You are a loving God, and You are very near to me. Let me trust You that I will again feel You in my life.

I ask this in the name of Jesus Christ.

Amen

Prayer for Overcoming Spiritual Doubts

Heavenly Father,

There are things I just don't understand about You. Why do children have to suffer? Why do natural disasters take so many lives? Why do people who do tremendous evil seem to thrive in this world? Now is a time in my life when I am encountering spiritual doubts, and I don't like the feeling.

Part of my problem is that I am not taking full responsibility for what I choose to focus on. I can choose to focus on Your blessings that surround me, or I can choose to focus on the things I don't understand. I am not choosing wisely, and I am paying the price spiritually.

The reality is that in this life we are looking through an opaque glass—things aren't clear and fully understandable—and they never will be in this life. Help me to focus on the gifts you have given me—gifts about which there can be no doubts because I experience them—see them, touch them, hear them....

Lord, let me be wise in my focus.

I ask this through Jesus Christ.

Amen.

Prayer for Ending Frustration with Christians/Church

Heavenly Father,

I am very frustrated with the behavior of Christians and the superficiality of the Church. It seems that we dress up for Sunday, put on our fake smiles, and pretend everything is wonderful. We give the appearance of caring, but we never get significantly involved in each other's lives. I am tired of this. It isn't what is described in the New Testament as the Christian community.

I know I am making myself frustrated and disappointed because I internally demand that Christians and the Church be different than they are. I never take into account that we are all subjects of the Fall—messy people in a messy church.

Rather than become frustrated and discouraged, through Your help may I accept reality—not like it, but accept it. Then help me to be the best Christian I can be—loving others patiently; praying for them; modeling for them, rather than exasperating myself about what they do or do not do.

Help me to see my own mess rather than focus on the mess of others. I certainly have enough to keep me busy for the rest of my life.

Lord, remind me that non-Christians will know we are Christians by our love, not by our perfection. Help me to love more perfectly and to forgive others when they fail to do what I am trying to do.

Through Christ our Lord,

Amen

Prayer When Experiencing a Major Loss

Heavenly Father,

I have experienced a major loss and I am feeling really low. My thoughts are all jumbled up and are unhelpful. I keep thinking that this loss should never have taken place and that I can't stand it. These thoughts just keep pulling me deeper and deeper into a dark pit.

Lord, help me to know and accept that many bad things happen in life. This is just what life is like. There is no reason why I should be spared significant losses. More importantly, help me to believe deep in my heart that I can and will stand this loss because You are with me, ready to comfort me if I will only cooperate with You. I may never be happy about the loss, but I will get through it, and life will again feel full of mercy and purpose.

Lord, help me to spend time each day using all my senses to remind me of all Your blessings which You pour around me.

You are my rock, my salvation, my comfort in times of sadness. You are my hope, my meaning, and my purpose.

I ask all this through Your Son, Jesus Christ.

Amen

Prayer for Solutions to Family Problems

Heavenly Father,

There are so many different kinds of family problems—poor communication as a couple, emotional abuse, addictions, behavioral problems with children, financial stresses, illness, and so on. I never thought I would experience a family problem, but I am right in the middle of one. I keep telling myself that I can't stand it any longer because it is so awful. I have not realized that I have the thought that I can't stand it any longer, but the reality is that I am standing it. The real truth is that I just don't like this situation and I wouldn't wish it on anyone. When I keep telling myself that I can't stand it anymore, I just feel overwhelmed and at times ready to give up, or I get angry, frustrated, or a combination of feelings.

Your holy word tells us that as we think in our heart so are we. It is the way we are thinking that causes our misery. I know I won't be happy about the family problem. That is simply too much to ask of me. However, there is a big difference between not being happy about the problem and being miserable. The problem is real; the misery I am making.

Lord, support me as I move to accept better thoughts—ones that do not cause me to become overwhelmed, but instead help me to realize that I can tolerate this situation with your help. Help me also to realize that no matter what happens in my family, life is meaningful, purposeful, and filled with beauty— even when I am not focusing on the meaning, purpose, or beauty.

Thank you for blessing me with a family.

I lift up all of this to you in the name of Jesus. Amen!

Prayer for Dealing with Chronic Health Problems

Heavenly Father,

You know that I am experiencing a chronic health problem and that I am often depressed and feel miserable about it. Like Jeremiah in Lamentations 3, in the bad times I tell myself that I am in darkness without light and that You, God, do not comfort me. I repeat these thoughts over and over again, which is what truly causes my misery.

Help me to take the step of Jeremiah to remind myself that daily you shower mercies and blessings on me. When I dwell on these realities, I will have hope over time.

Lord, help me also not to isolate myself from others, but to talk to others about my hope. And when I do talk to others, have me talk about that hope rather than exclusively talking about my problems.

Allow me to see that while my chronic health problem is very real, it does not define my life, nor is it the sum total of the reality of my life.

Thank you for being a caring God even in the midst of my health problem.

I ask all these things in the name of Jesus.

Amen.

Prayer to Overcome a Judgmental Spirit

Heavenly Father,

I know that Your Son told us not to judge lest we be judged, but I am finding myself judging people very harshly lately. I do not like this about myself and I don't like the results of doing this. It makes me hateful toward others, sometimes feeling superior, and just, overall, making me feel negative about the people around me. I know that my judgmentalism comes out of some ungodly demands that I have toward others, namely, that they don't measure up to my standards or God's standards. I think that I can't stand it when they don't seem to even want to measure up to good standards. I know that the problem isn't the standards, but me and my demands that others must live up to those standards. I forget that none of us has lived up to Your standards because we are all a mess.

I pray for your help to move from demandingness to accepting others unconditionally. I may not like their failures, but I can stand them, and I can love those who fail just as You love me with all my failures.

Help me also to become aware of these unhelpful thoughts earlier so I can stop them and refrain from the judgmentalism.

I live only by Your grace and trust that I can overcome this negative spirit of judgmentalism.

Through Christ the Lord,

Amen

Prayer When Feeling Hurt about the Past

Father,

I had a difficult past growing up and beyond and today I continue to feel very bad about that past and believe that I am damaged as a result of it. I focus too much on the past and too little on my present with You and the wonderful plan that You have for my life. I am tired of giving the past more power over me than Your grace in my life. This feeling of hurt negatively impacts my life in so many ways—I tend not to trust people who are nice to me thinking that they will hurt me and disappoint me, I isolate myself and end up feeling lonely, I have made my world very small thinking that I could not handle one more hurt in my life.

Lord, help me to put my past in proper perspective. There were bad things that happened, but they do not determine who I am and what my future could be. Let me see myself as You see me—Your child, an ambassador for You to others, a witness to Your saving grace.

Let me focus on others and how I can help them rather than so much on me and my negative past. In that way I can serve You by serving others who are hurting.

I turn my life over to You and work with You to have more hope.

In the precious name of Jesus,

Amen

Prayer for Dealing with a Bad Work Environment

Heavenly Father,

My work environment is toxic. There is so much negativity— no one cooperates, people tend to be negative and just want to do as little as they can and get out as quickly as they are able, and the whole situation is very tense. I am tense. I make myself even tenser by telling myself that I can't stand it there another day. This tension is invading the rest of my life. I have trouble sleeping, I get headaches, and I feel muscle tension a good amount of the time. It is exhausting me and I find myself complaining about it too much to my friends. I know they are tired of listening to me. I am tired of listening to me complain about. I wish I used that time to praise You.

Lord, I need Your help to see the bad work environment in a different light. I would love it if I could see that You have put me in that place to be a support to others and a person of hope to those who do not know You. Your Word says that your mercies and blessings are new every morning. Help me to take them into my work and be a mercy to others.

With You I can stand my workplace and realize that it is negative but in no way does it have the power to make my whole life seem negative. It is a "slight momentary affliction" in which I can have hope if I continue to control my thoughts with diligence and patience.

I thank You for how You will work in my life as I cooperate with You.

I ask this in the precious name of Jesus.

Amen

Prayer for Overcoming Sin and Temptation

Father in heaven,

At times it seems that I am surrounded by temptations and that I am too weak to stand up to them. It seems that they are too big, too powerful, and I am too small, and too weak. Help me see that it is not about how big I am, but about how big You are. Putting myself down doesn't help me in any way, and in fact, it just sets me up to sin again. Help me stop telling myself that I can't stand this temptation and all my sins.

See how focused I am on me and the challenges in my life. Help me shift that focus to Your steadfast love in the midst of the temptations. Let me see the temptations as occasions when I can trust You to get me through. Remind me share the triumphs over sin and temptation with other people who similarly struggle.

I like it when Paul says that he has found resources in himself to handle all things through You. That is my wish for me and my prayer to You. I want to take your Word and let it become so much a part of my life that it is a powerful resource in times of temptation.

I praise You and thank You for Your Holy Word and Your constant support.

Through Christ my Lord,

Amen

Prayer for Those Who Had an Abortion

Heavenly Father,

I had an abortion and now I am feeling terribly guilty, spiritually damaged, and as though what I have done makes me completely and utterly unacceptable to You--that I am beyond forgiveness. This is making me feel depressed a good amount of the time. It even has me avoid going to church because when I am in church I think about what I did and often I begin to cry uncontrollably. I feel like I will never get over this.

There are moments when I read in the Bible that nothing can separate me from Your love. That just seems too good to be true and that this particular action of mine is so bad that You have no choice but to reject me forever.

Help me to accept the truth of Your Word and believe in my heart that You will never let me be separated from You and Your love. When I start dwelling on what I did, lift me up and give me the strength to remind myself that I am Your child and that You will love me forever.

I pray that someday I will find ways to help the children of this world, starting with the children in my community. I pray that the way to help becomes clear to me and that a way opens for me to serve you by serving children.

I ask this in the precious name of Jesus.

Amen

Prayer to Overcome Resentment

Heavenly Father,

I am making myself feel resentful about something that someone did to me. I hate this feeling. I read somewhere that resentment is like eating rat poison and hoping that the rat will die. I know the feeling because my resentment seems to be eating me alive. My resentment doesn't help me and it certainly doesn't help what the other person did to me or increase the possibility that the person changes. It is a total waste of time.

I want to move beyond that negative feeling and embrace disappointment about what was done to me, but not get caught up in the debilitating resentment. I know that I have disappointed You many times by my actions, but You just respond in love, a quiet love that is so powerful. I pray that I can come to that point and follow what You have modeled toward me. Help me pray for the person, transform my thinking about them, and act only out of love. I hope that it can be a challenge in our relationship that we can discuss and overcome to create an even better relationship.

Thank You so much for being You and I praise You for all Your wonderful traits and most of all for Your constant love and support.

In the name of Jesus,

Amen

Prayer for Overcoming Financial Challenges

Dear Father in Heaven,

My family and I are going through a rough financial period. Money is very tight and I wonder whether we will be able to pay the bills. I worry about this day and night, but I also try to make sure that the children do not see my worry, but it is now becoming difficult to hide my emotions. I know I am to cast my anxiety on You, but sometimes I just don't know how to do that. I think I have cast it on You and then I seem to take it back and worry again. I go to bed worrying about it and I wake up worrying about it. It is putting a strain on my marriage and my mind is so focused on the financial situation that I can't think very clearly about what to do about it.

The "what if's" fill my mind. I ask for your help to drive them from my mind so that I trust in your plan for me and my family and that we will get through this. I don't pretend to know what You want me to learn from this situation, but it is comforting to know that although I don't know, You are with me. It reminds me of how You were with Job throughout his material losses.

We do not live on bread or money alone. I live by Your grace. Help me remember that when my focus is so much on the bread and money.

I put this matter in Your hands and I will get busy doing what You would have me do.

All of this I ask in the name of Jesus.

Amen

Prayers When Coveting Someone Else's Possessions

Heavenly Father,

[Insert name] has something that I want very badly. I know that coveting is breaking one of the Ten Commandments, but I am still doing it. I don't like that I am doing it, and I beat myself up that I am doing it, but I am doing it nonetheless. I know exactly my ungodly thinking in this case and it is that I deserve to have what they have, and I should have it.

I can't believe that after all the blessings You have given me that I am so ungrateful and unsatisfied that I am dwelling on having this one thing. It would be bad enough if I just had the thought once, but I am dwelling on it and it makes me feel empty, envious, unfulfilled, and jealous. Those emotions are not pretty and they in no way glorify You.

It would be helpful if I quit focusing on how entitled I am and how I need what I really don't need. Every time I catch myself coveting, please redirect my thoughts to how much You have really blessed me. It may be hard but my prayer is that I come to be happy for [Insert name] and the fact that they have what they have.

I ask this in the name of Jesus.

Amen

Prayers to Stop Gossiping

Dear Heavenly Father,

I know that You said in Your Holy Word that the tongue is the hardest part of us to tame. While my tongue should form words praising You and uplifting and helping others, I am using mine far too much to gossip about others. Way too often my gossip is just a form of backbiting, which is ugly and impedes my spiritual growth. Gossiping can be so insidious because it divides the community, puts a fellow human in a bad light, and creates doubt in the mind of others about the individual. It clearly has no redeeming purpose and serves no positive function.

I am not sure what my unhelpful beliefs are that cause me to gossip, but I wonder whether I think that I must look good to others and that a way to do this is to make others look bad. The reality is that I make others look bad and I look worse. I would like to change my thoughts to wishes that we all care for each other such that we speak kind and uplifting words about each other and thereby strength community. I would appreciate Your help in actually changing my thoughts for the better.

This I ask in the precious name of Jesus.

Amen

Prayer for Our Political Leaders

Heavenly Father,

I caught myself recently saying some very negative words about my political leaders. While I firmly believe that some of them are not doing what I would like them to do for this country, I am not helping in any way by bad mouthing them. What is worse is that I watch the news that repeats and reinforces by negative thinking and I surround myself with people who share my political beliefs and together we backbite and criticize those with whom we do not agree.

What is this within me that has me not only do this, but enjoy doing it and, at times, has me feel superior to those who do not agree with me. Lord, please help me to take to heart Your Word in which Your Son directs us to take the log from my own eye before I concern myself so much with the speck in another person's eye. The log in my eye prevents me from seeing any good in the politicians with whom I do not agree. Help me get serious about my spiritual growth and stop this negativity. Help me to pray for all politicians because if they succeed according to Your will, then we all succeed and will be blessed. Help me to overcome this childish tribalism in which I get engaged.

Instead of thinking that those politicians must change, help me to have a godly desire about this.

I ask this in the precious and beautiful name of Jesus.

Amen

Prayer to Overcome a Poor Attitude Toward Non-Christians

Heavenly Father,

I am so sorry that I hold such negative views of those who do not share my faith. I get caught up in thinking that Buddhists, Muslims, Hindus, Atheists, and other non-Christians must be stupid or silly to believe in what they believe. I think that they should see the superiority of my faith and leave their own. I look down upon them, get condescending toward them, and dismiss the seriousness with which they hold their views. Help me to disagree with their faith but to do so with love, patience, and kindness. Keep me away from a superior attitude, which surely must come across in my dealings with them. I think of Your loving attitude toward the Ninevites during the time of Jonah and the ways in which my attitude toward non-Christians is much more like Jonah's negative attitude toward the Ninevites than Your attitude.

It boils down the fact that I am putting them down in my mind. Instead of putting them down, help me to hold them up, love them, and show Your light to them through my love.

My prayer is that someday all knees will bow to Your name, but until then, let my knee bow in reverence toward You and my actions reflect Your goodness.

As always, I ask this in the precious name of Jesus.

Amen

Conclusion

The flexibility of REBT and the fact that it does not attack Christian clients' values or goals, but only their irrational beliefs about those values and goals, make it a potentially powerful and effective form of psychotherapy with Christian clients who are open to it. Moreover, the ability to incorporate into REBT those religious beliefs and practices most meaningful to Christian clients, maximizes the possibility of achieving profound changes in the clients' philosophy of life and thereby decreasing their emotional pain and suffering and self-defeating behaviors. REBT, possibly more than any other form of psychotherapy, increases the likelihood that the clients will, the in the words of St. Paul, be "a new creation," for whom "everything old has passed away" and "everything has become new."

References

Armstrong, D. M. (1973) <u>Belief, truth and knowledge</u>. Cambridge: Cambridge University Press, 3.

Craigie, F.D. and Tan, S.Y. (1989) Changing resistant assumptions in Christian cognitive-behavioral therapy. <u>Journal of Psychology and Theology</u>, 17, 98.

Ellis, A. (1993) The advantages and disadvantages of self-help therapy materials. <u>Professional Psychology: Research and Practice</u>, 24, 336.

Lawrence, C. (1987) Rational emotive therapy and the religious client. <u>Journal of Rational-Emotive Therapy</u>, 5, 19.

Peirce, C.S. (1995) The fixation of belief. In <u>Philosophical Writings of Peirce</u>, (Ed.) by Justus Buchler. New York: Dover Publication, 10.

Stoop, D. (1997) <u>Self-talk: Key to personal growth</u>. Grand Rapids, MI: Fleming H. Revell.

West, G.F. and Reynolds, J. (Summer 1997) The applicability of selected rational-emotive therapy principles for pastoral counseling. <u>The Journal of Pastoral Care</u>, 187-194.

Additional Resources

Additional information about Rational Emotive Behavior Therapy can be found at the website for the Albert Ellis Institute: http://www.rebt.org. Through the store at this website one can find and purchase helpful books, CD's, DVD's, pamphlets, and a list of upcoming public workshops and lectures. The Institute offers reasonably priced individual and group therapy. It also offers training for psychotherapists who would like to learn REBT.

The Albert Ellis Institute is located at 145 East 42nd Street, 9th Floor, New York City, NY. Their telephone number is 212.535.0822.

The author of this book is a Fellow, Approved Supervisor, and Diplomate in CBT/REBT through the Albert Ellis Institute.

Made in the USA
Columbia, SC
14 September 2020